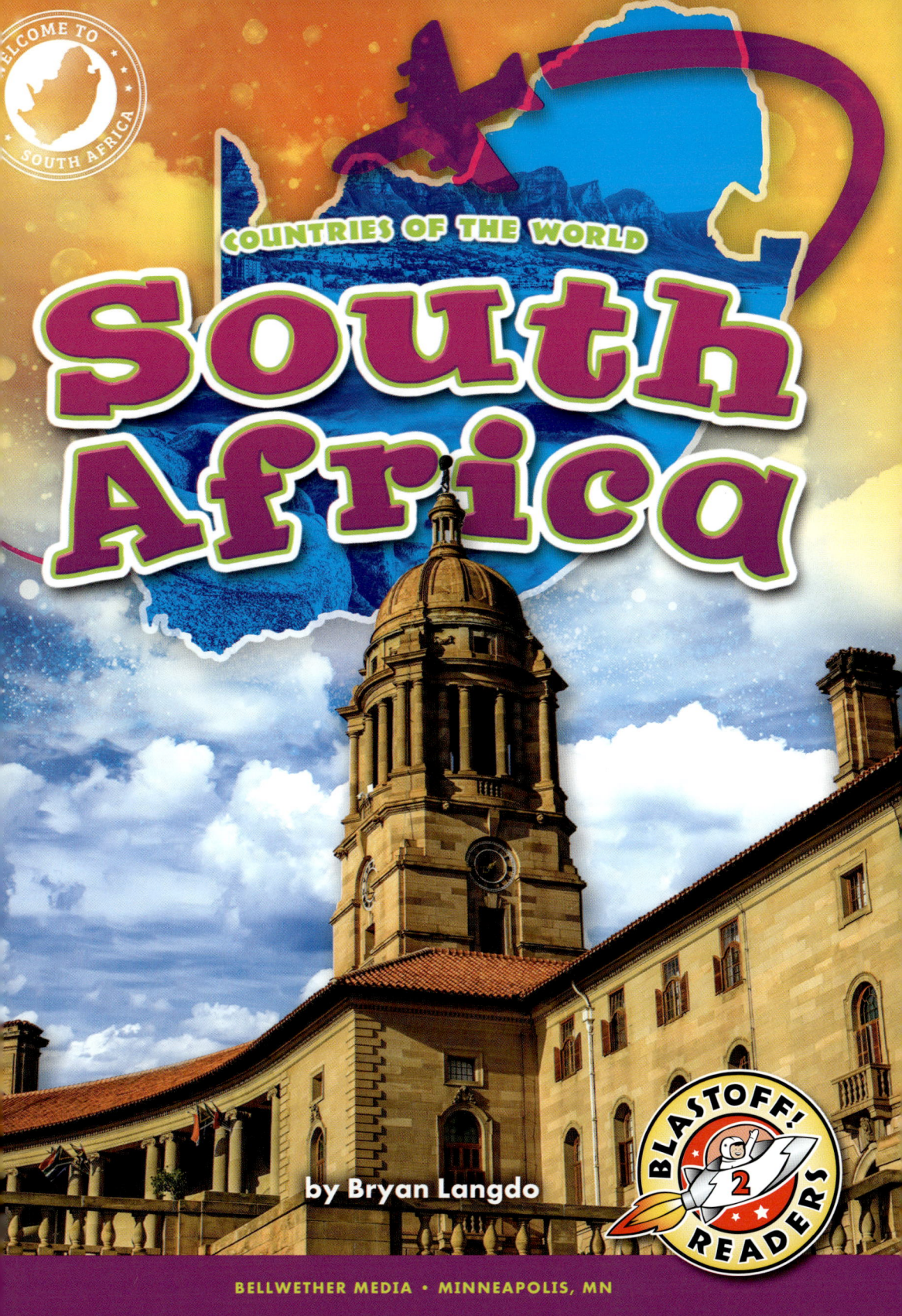

Blastoff! Readers are carefully developed by literacy experts to build reading stamina and move students toward fluency by combining standards-based content with developmentally appropriate text.

Level 1 provides the most support through repetition of high-frequency words, light text, predictable sentence patterns, and strong visual support.

Level 2 offers early readers a bit more challenge through varied sentences, increased text load, and text-supportive special features.

Level 3 advances early-fluent readers toward fluency through increased text load, less reliance on photos, advancing concepts, longer sentences, and more complex special features.

★ **Blastoff! Universe**

Reading Level — Grade K → Grades 1–3 → Grade 4

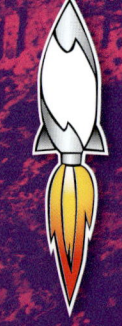

This edition first published in 2025 by Bellwether Media, Inc.

No part of this publication may be reproduced in whole or in part without written permission of the publisher. For information regarding permission, write to Bellwether Media, Inc., Attention: Permissions Department, 6012 Blue Circle Drive, Minnetonka, MN 55343.

Library of Congress Cataloging-in-Publication Data

Names: Langdo, Bryan, author.
Title: South Africa / by Bryan Langdo.
Other titles: Blastoff! readers. 2, Countries of the world.
Description: Minneapolis, MN : Bellwether Media, Inc., 2025. | Series: Blastoff! readers. Countries of the world | Includes bibliographical references and index. | Audience: Ages 5-8 | Audience: Grades 2-3 | Summary: "Relevant images match informative text in this introduction to South Africa. Intended for students in kindergarten through third grade"– Provided by publisher.
Identifiers: LCCN 2024039289 (print) | LCCN 2024039290 (ebook) | ISBN 9798893042344 (library binding) | ISBN 9798893043310 (ebook)
Subjects: LCSH: South Africa–Juvenile literature.
Classification: LCC DT1719 .L36 2025 (print) | LCC DT1719 (ebook) | DDC 968–dc23/eng/20240826
LC record available at https://lccn.loc.gov/2024039289
LC ebook record available at https://lccn.loc.gov/2024039290

Text copyright © 2025 by Bellwether Media, Inc. BLASTOFF! READERS and associated logos are trademarks and/or registered trademarks of Bellwether Media, Inc.

Editor: Suzane Nguyen   Designer: Laura Sowers

Printed in the United States of America, North Mankato, MN.

Table of Contents

All About South Africa   4
Land and Animals   6
Life in South Africa   12
South Africa Facts   20
Glossary   22
To Learn More   23
Index   24

All About South Africa

Cape Town

South Africa is in southern Africa. It has three capital cities. They are Bloemfontein, Cape Town, and Pretoria.

The country is called "rainbow nation." It is home to many **cultures**.

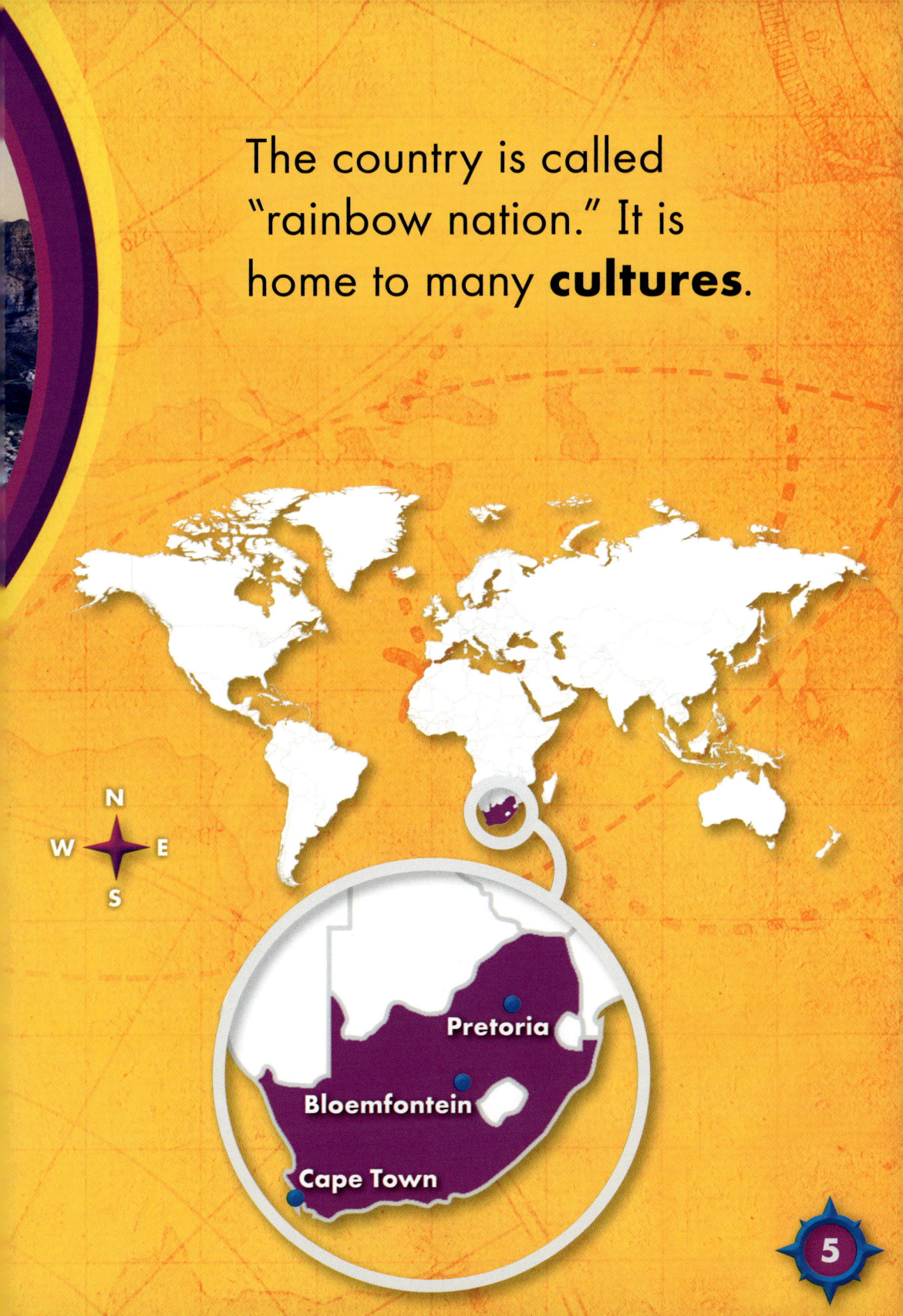

Land and Animals

A high **plateau** covers most of South Africa. **Deserts** sit in the west.

Mountains rise to the east, west, and south. Table Mountain stands near Cape Town.

desert

Table Mountain

Size: 3,563 feet (1,086 meters) tall

Famous For: home to many plants and animals, and a popular place for hiking and camping

South Africa is mostly **temperate**. It is dry and warm.

The country gets very little rain. Snow falls in the mountains.

South Africa has a lot of wildlife. Elephants eat leaves off trees. Springboks leap high!

African savanna elephant

Blue cranes lay their eggs by water. At night, lions hunt!

Life in South Africa

South Africans come from different **backgrounds**. Most South Africans are Black.

The country has 11 main languages. Zulu and Xhosa are most commonly spoken.

The arts are important in South Africa. Musicians may mix jazz, pop, and **traditional** music.

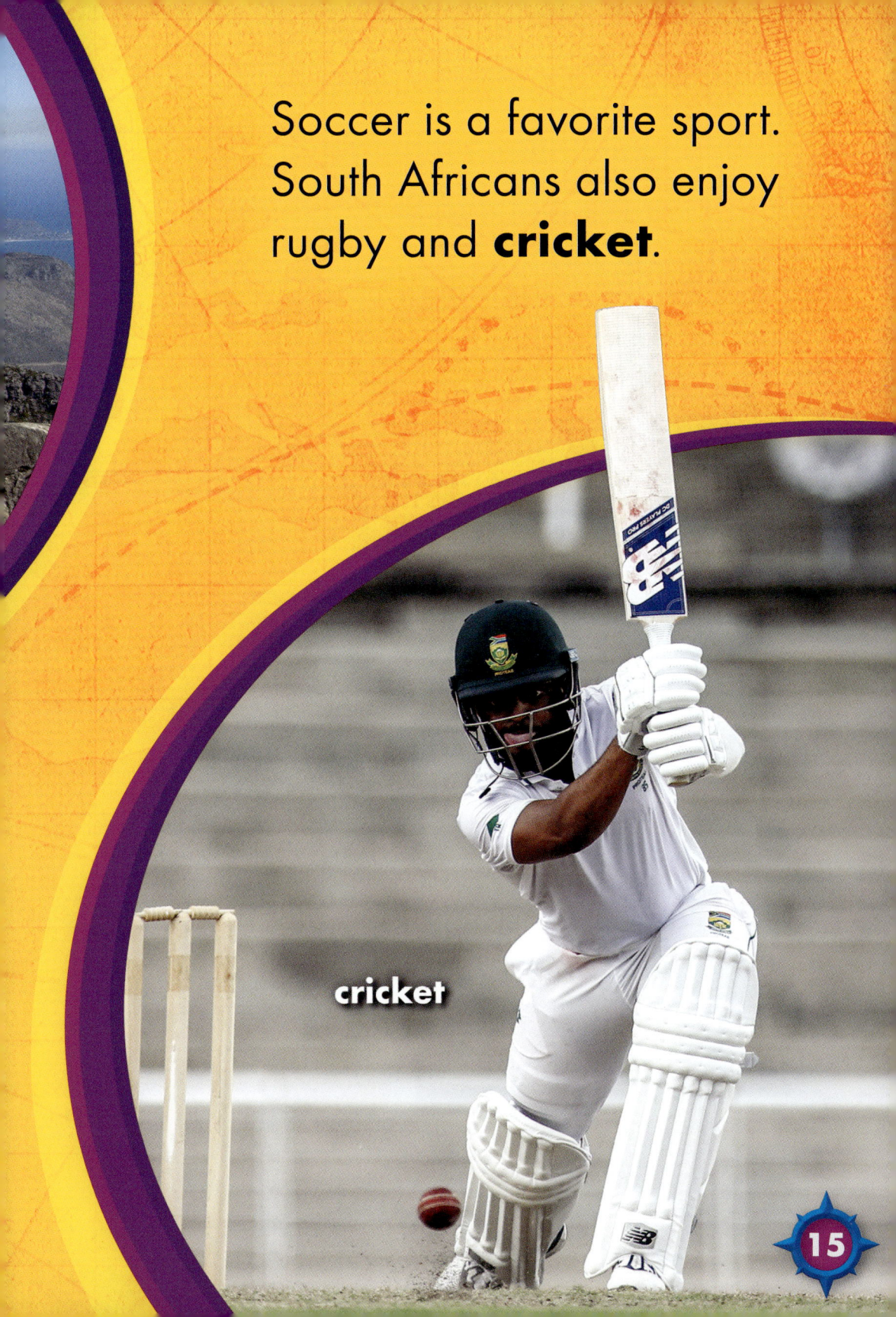

Soccer is a favorite sport. South Africans also enjoy rugby and **cricket**.

cricket

Bobotie is a baked dish. It has meat and **curry** spices. *Mashonzha* is dried caterpillars!

South African Foods

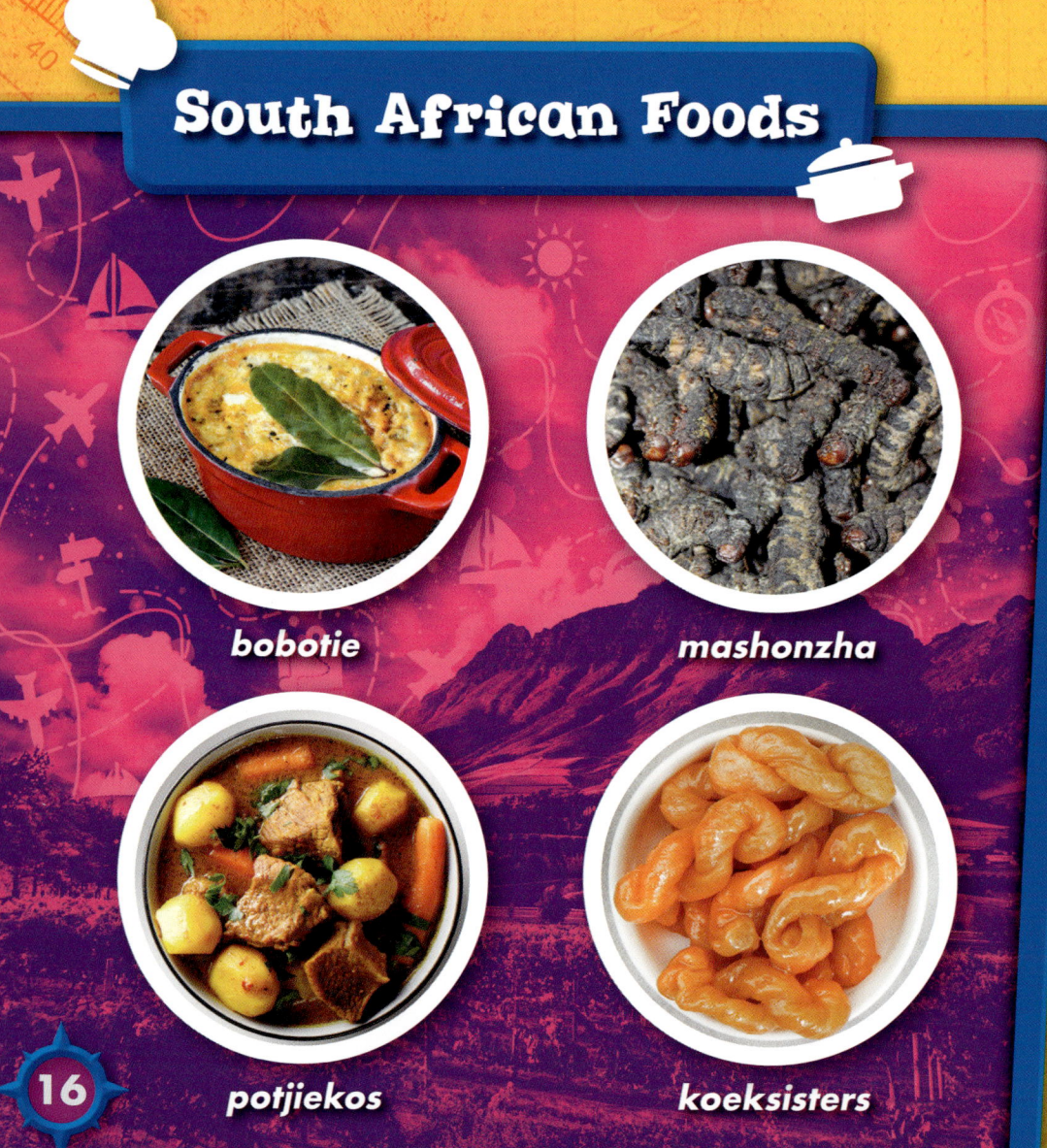

bobotie

mashonzha

potjiekos

koeksisters

Potjiekos is a tasty stew.
Koeksisters are sweet fried dough.

April 27 is Freedom Day. People share food with family and friends.

Heritage Day is September 24. People enjoy barbecues, parades, and music. They **celebrate** their **diverse** country!

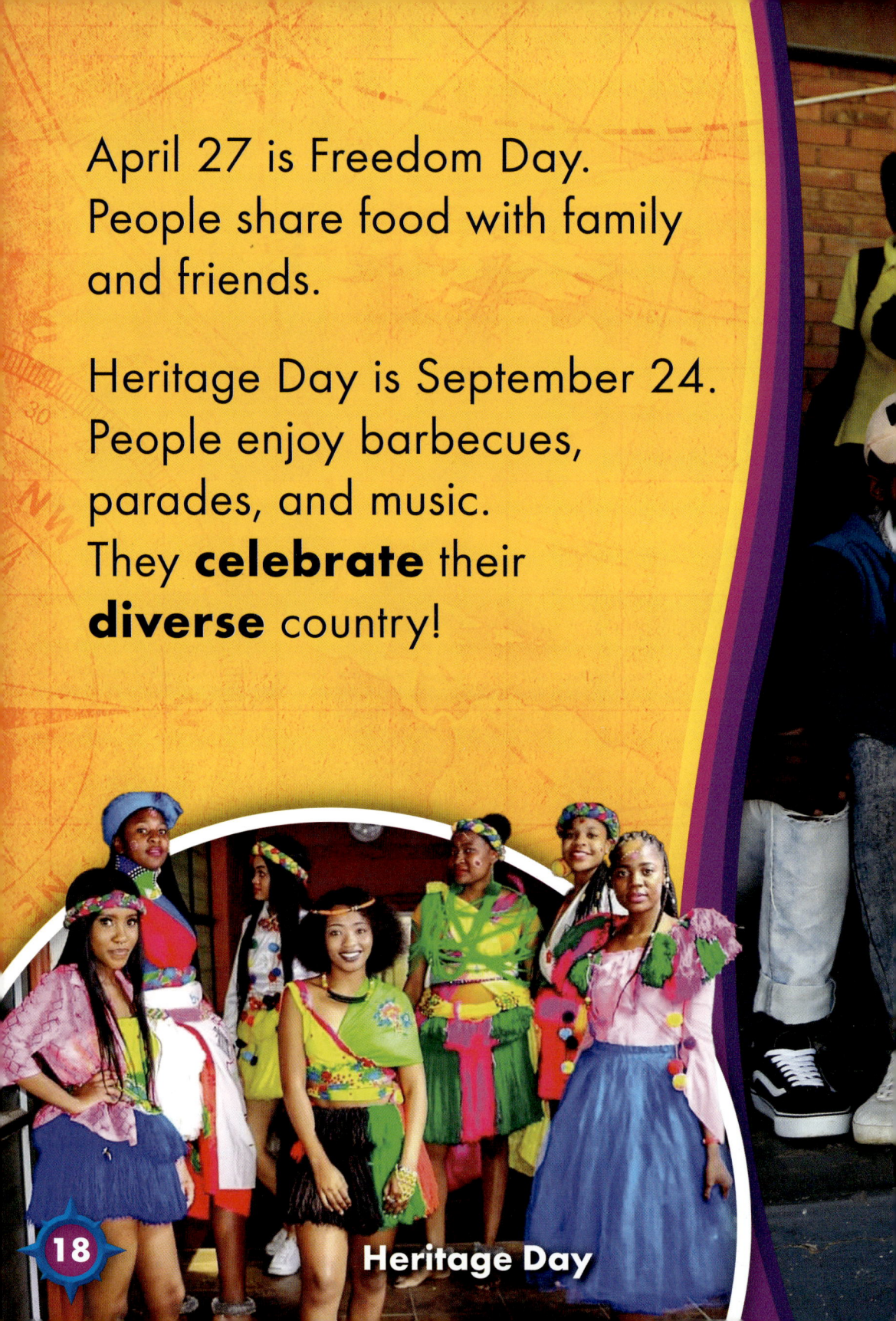

Heritage Day

Freedom Day

South Africa Facts

Size: 470,693 square miles (1,219,090 square kilometers)

Population: 60,442,647 (2024)

National Holiday: Freedom Day (April 27)

Main Languages: Zulu, Xhosa, and 9 others

Capital Cities: Bloemfontein, Cape Town, and Pretoria

Famous Face

Name: Trevor Noah

Famous For: an award-winning comedian, TV host, and writer

Religions

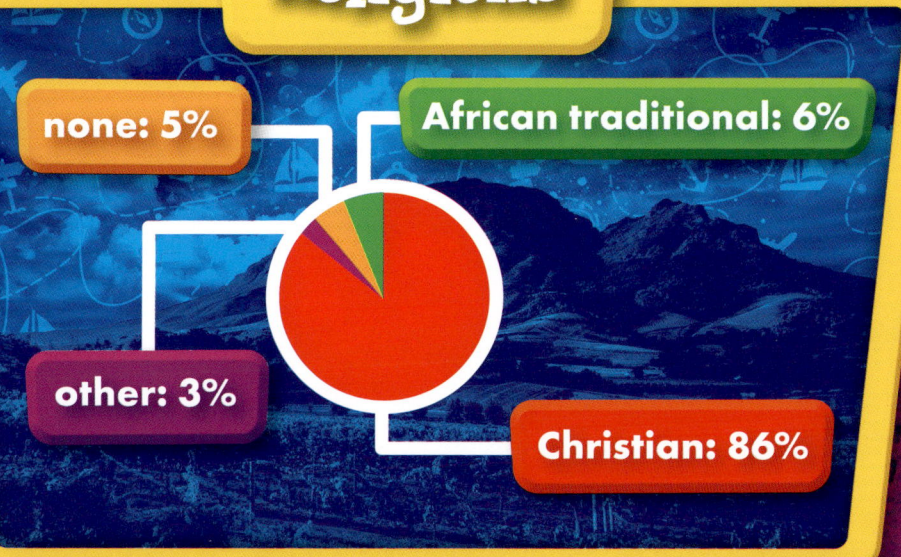

- none: 5%
- African traditional: 6%
- other: 3%
- Christian: 86%

Top Landmarks

Cradle of Humankind

Kruger National Park

Union Buildings

Glossary

backgrounds—people's experiences, knowledge and family histories

celebrate—to do something special or fun for an event, occasion, or holiday

cricket—a field game similar to baseball that is played with a bat and a ball

cultures—the beliefs, arts, and ways of life in a place or society

curry—a combination of spices, like pepper, coriander, cumin, turmeric, and fenugreek seeds

deserts—dry lands with few plants and little rainfall

diverse—made up of people whose backgrounds or identities are different from each other

plateau—a flat, raised area of land

temperate—related to weather that is not too hot or too cold

traditional—related to customs, ideas, or beliefs handed down from one generation to the next

To Learn More

AT THE LIBRARY

Mather, Charis. *A Visit to South Africa*. Minneapolis, Minn.: Bearport Publishing, 2024.

Schuh, Mari. *Animals of the African Savanna*. North Mankato, Minn.: Capstone Publishing, 2022.

Spanier, Kristine. *South Africa*. Minneapolis, Minn.: Jump!, 2020.

ON THE WEB

FACTSURFER

Factsurfer.com gives you a safe, fun way to find more information.

1. Go to www.factsurfer.com.

2. Enter "South Africa" into the search box and click 🔍.

3. Select your book cover to see a list of related content.

Index

Africa, 4
animals, 10, 11
Bloemfontein, 4, 5
Cape Town, 4, 5, 6
capital (see Bloemfontein, Cape Town, and Pretoria)
cricket, 15
cultures, 5
deserts, 6
food, 16, 17, 18
Freedom Day, 18, 19
Heritage Day, 18
languages, 12
map, 5
mountains, 6, 7, 9
music, 14, 18
nickname, 5
people, 12, 14, 15, 18
plateau, 6
Pretoria, 4, 5

rain, 9
rugby, 15
say hello, 13
snow, 9
soccer, 15
South Africa facts, 20–21
Table Mountain, 6, 7
Xhosa, 12
Zulu, 12, 13

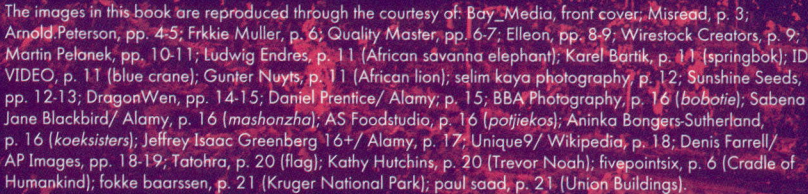

The images in this book are reproduced through the courtesy of: Bay_Media, front cover; Misread, p. 3; Arnold.Peterson, pp. 4-5; Frkkie Muller, p. 6; Quality Master, pp. 6-7; Elleon, pp. 8-9; Wirestock Creators, p. 9; Martin Pelanek, pp. 10-11; Ludwig Endres, p. 11 (African savanna elephant); Karel Bartik, p. 11 (springbok); ID-VIDEO, p. 11 (blue crane); Gunter Nuyts, p. 11 (African lion); selim kaya photography, p. 12; Sunshine Seeds, pp. 12-13; DragonWen, pp. 14-15; Daniel Prentice/ Alamy, p. 15; BBA Photography, p. 16 (*bobotie*); Sabena Jane Blackbird/ Alamy, p. 16 (*mashonzha*); AS Foodstudio, p. 16 (*potjiekos*); Aninka Bongers-Sutherland, p. 16 (*koeksisters*); Jeffrey Isaac Greenberg 16+/ Alamy, p. 17; Unique9/ Wikipedia, p. 18; Denis Farrell/ AP Images, pp. 18-19; Tatohra, p. 20 (flag); Kathy Hutchins, p. 20 (Trevor Noah); fivepointsix, p. 6 (Cradle of Humankind); fokke baarssen, p. 21 (Kruger National Park); paul saad, p. 21 (Union Buildings).